Birthright

Songbook

Songs & Scripts for Worship

lillenas
PUBLISHING COMPANY

Contents

Birthright

WHAT IS BIRTHRIGHT?

Birthright can be so much more than just a group of great worship songs. Birthright was created to be an interactive, multi-sensory worship experience that takes a congregation into a rediscovery of their Christian legacy. It was created with the aim of using many artistic forms to communicate with the audience the truth of our legacy in Christ. It was also intended to be a medium through which the audience could worship the Almighty. It's all about authentic worship through song, video, Scripture reading, drama, art, Communion, and more.

The full production was created in the spring of 2005 by a team of worship leaders and artists. The various media resources (music, drama, video, etc) were captured on a production DVD that is intended to aid the local congregation in reproducing this multi-layered experience.

The DVD provides everything you need: drama scripts along with a video demo and training; MP3's featuring three types of tracks for each song, worship music lead sheets, over ten background video loops, customizable worship outlines, production maps, photos and extensive notes, the video Faces of Christ for use during Communion, and more.

The Birthright Production DVD is available where Christian resources are available or directly from Lillenas at Lillenas.com or by calling 1-800-877-0700.

He Reigns

Words and Music by
PETER FURLER and
STEVE TAYLOR

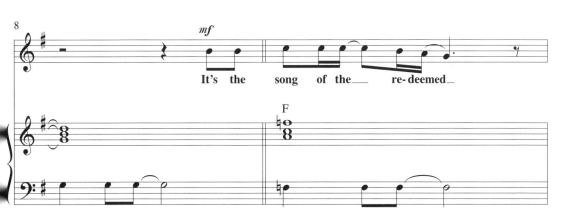

ris - ing from_ the Af - ri - can plain._

It's the song of the_ for-giv - en_

drown - ing out_ the Am - a - zon rain._

The song of As - ian_ be-liev - ers

hal - le - lu - jah! He reigns,____ He reigns."

It's all God's chil - dren sing - ing, "Glo - ry, glo - ry,

CD: 3

hal - le - lu - jah! He reigns,____ He reigns."____

And let it rise a - bove__ the four____ winds,

some were_ meant_ to per - sist._

Of all the bells_ rung from a thou - sand_ stee - ples,

none rings_ tru-er_ than this:_

It's all God's chil-dren sing-ing, "Glo - ry, glo - ry,

50
hal - le - lu - jah! He reigns,_____ He reigns."
C   G

52
It's all God's chil-dren sing-ing, "Glo - ry, glo - ry,
G   F

54
CD: 5 2nd time
1
hal - le - lu - jah! He reigns,_____ He reigns."
C   G

56
(to pg. 10, meas. 49)
2
It's all God's chil-dren sing-ing,_____ He reigns."
G   G

He reigns." It's all God's chil - dren sing - ing,
hal - le - lu - jah,
hal - le - lu - jah!

"Glo - ry, glo - ry, hal - le - lu - jah! He reigns."
Glo - ry, glo - ry, hal - le - lu - jah! He reigns,

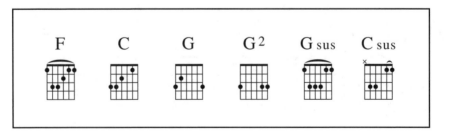

F   C   G   G 2   G sus   C sus

The Noise We Make

Words and Music by
CHRIS TOMLIN and
JESSE REEVES

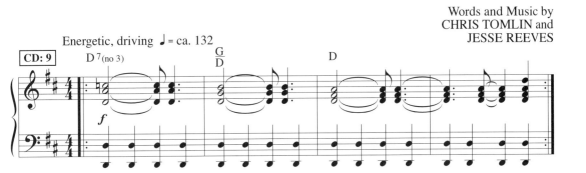

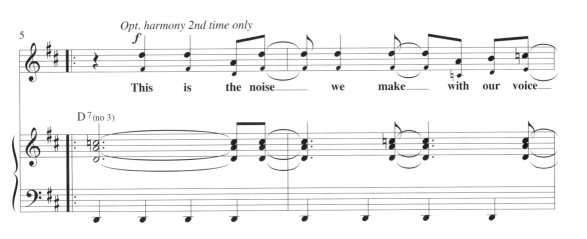

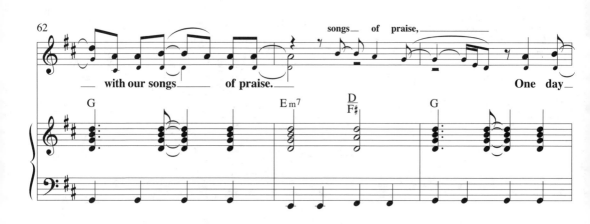

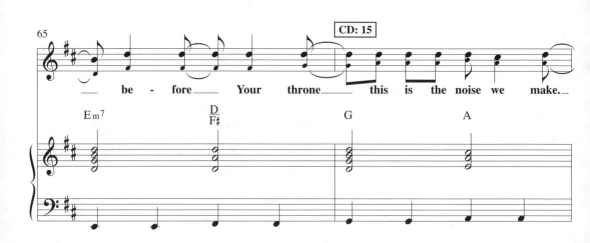

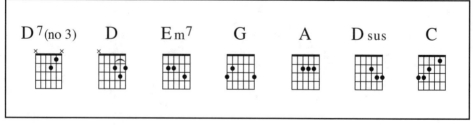

Storm

by one**time**blind

Running Time: Approximately 8 minutes

Theme: Everyone has a place and a purpose, and it's only when that purpose is used as God intended that the story is made complete.

Scripture References: Psalm 27:14, 138:8; Jeremiah 29:11 (NIV)

Synopsis: Two friends are talking about God's timing and will for a particular situation. To illustrate a point, the first friend asks for volunteers from the audience and proceeds to give each person, including his friend, a task and instructions. He begins to tell a story, pointing to each person as his or her turn comes to participate. The second friend interrupts the story with his out-of-place tasks. Finally, he does it as instructed and a beautiful storm is recreated. After the volunteers leave, the two friends finish their conversation by learning that "everything has a place, even in a storm."

Cast: TONY
        DREW
        THREE AUDIENCE MEMBERS

Props: One chair

Setting: TONY and DREW walk on-stage having a conversation

DREW *(sighing)*: Ugh. You know what I'm saying? I'm just really frustrated now.

TONY *(confused)*: Not really.

DREW *(frustrated)*: I mean, it's kind of like-I've got all of these great plans, you know? And all of this energy, and I'm ready to use it, but God is not letting me do it.

TONY: Well, maybe it's what you just said-you have all these plans.

DREW: Yeah, I do!

TONY: Maybe it's the way you're approaching it. Maybe you should wait. Wait until the Lord gives you the green light to do the things He wants you to do.

DREW: But I feel like He already has. I mean, He should have. I've got the excitement, the intensity, the energy, and I'm ready to go-but every time I try, it falls apart. It's not making sense to me. It should just happen!

TONY: OK, I truly believe the Lord has a plan for you, Drew.

DREW: Yeah.

TONY: And I believe He has a purpose in those things He's put on your heart. I believe He's going to let you do them, but maybe you're jumping ahead of His plan. Maybe some things need to happen before you carry them out.

DREW: But I want it to happen now. I'm ready now.

TONY: That's the point-the timing. I know its super frustrating, but the Lord designed life so that certain things have to happen before others.

DREW: Well, that doesn't really make sense to me.

TONY *(thinking)*: OK. Uh, I've got an idea. Maybe this will help clear things up for you. Why don't you step over there for a second? *(He moves DREW over to SL, instructing him to stand in a certain place.)* OK, um, I need some help here.

(TONY looks out into the audience. He chooses THREE AUDIENCE MEMBERS from different sections of the audience, calling them on-stage and placing them across the stage, one person SR, opposite from DREW, and the other two between them. He leaves enough space in between people so he can easily move between them. Once he gets everyone on-stage and in place, he introduces himself and asks the people their names. For script purposes, the audience members' names will be RYAN, LAURA, and KAT.)

TONY: OK, people. We're going to make a storm. I know it sounds weird, but stick with me. This is very cool. *(He moves to RYAN, the person at SR.)* OK, Ryan. This is going to be your part. You're the mighty wind. See this section over here? *(He points to the section of the audience in front of SR.)* They're going to be your friends. They're going to join you. So, this is how you do the wind. *(He demonstrates, rubbing the palms of his hands together.)* OK? Now, I'll motion to you when I want you to get louder and softer, all right?

(TONY *watches as* RYAN *practices, directing him to involve the audience, motioning him to get louder then softer, and then telling him to stop. He then moves on to* LAURA, *the next person.*)

TONY *(to* LAURA*)*: OK, you-you're the sprinkles. You're the start of the storm. You're going to snap your fingers like this. *(He snaps his fingers, alternating back and forth between hands.)* The same thing applies-get faster and slower when I motion to you. This is your section right here. *(He points to the section of the audience to the left of the last section.)* You will direct them.

(TONY *gets* LAURA *to practice directing the audience, then stops her. He moves on to* KAT, *who is next in line and standing just to the right of* DREW. *He grabs the chair and gives it to her to sit on.*)

TONY *(speaking to* KAT, *who is now sitting down)*: You're going to be a multi-tasker. You're going to be the main part of the storm. After the sprinkles, it starts to rain. This is how you do the rain. *(He slaps his hands on his thighs, getting* KAT *to imitate him.)* And then, you'll become a downpour. So your feet go on the floor, and you stomp them like this.

(TONY *demonstrates, getting* KAT *to imitate again. He directs her to do both at the same time and points out the next section of the audience for her to lead.* TONY *then moves on to* DREW.*)

TONY *(speaking to* DREW*)*: Drew.

DREW *(expectantly)*: Yeah. I'm ready, man.

TONY: All right, you are the mighty thunder.

DREW *(excited)*: That's right, I am.

TONY: So, you're the thunderclap. This is what you do. *(He claps his hands loudly, four times in succession, creating the sound of thunder and directing* DREW *to imitate him.)*

DREW *(practicing)*: All right! I'm a good clapper!

TONY *(pointing to the far left section of the audience)*: OK. This is your section. You'll lead them.

DREW: OK. (*He gets the audience to join him, practicing the thunderclaps.*)

TONY (*to everyone on-stage*): Now, this is the important part. When I cue you, either by pointing to you or touching you on the shoulder, that's when I want you to come in. And to make it complete, I'm going to tell a story!

(TONY *looks excitedly at everyone then begins his story in a "storytelling voice." This story can be adapted by anyone playing* TONY's *role.*)

TONY: All right, then, here we go! It was my grandma's birthday, and we spent the whole day at the park. We went down the slide, played on the swings, threw the football around. My grandma was stirring the potato salad when all of a sudden the wind picked up.

(TONY *is just about to tap* RYAN *on the shoulder to begin his part when* DREW *suddenly breaks in with loud clapping.*)

TONY (*stopping the story and addressing* DREW): Whoa, whoa. Drew! What are you doing?

DREW (*continuing his thunderclaps*): I'm practicing! I'm the thunder.

TONY: Yeah, I know you're the thunder. But you need to wait. It's not your time yet. When I cue you, that's when you come in.

DREW: I know; I was just practicing.

TONY: OK, but this is your purpose-when I cue you, you come in. OK? Now you're all practiced up. Here we go.

DREW: Fine. Yeah. OK.

TONY (*beginning his story again*): We spent the whole day at the park for my grandma's birthday. Going down the slide, playing on the swings, throwing the football. Grandma's stirring the potato salad and all of a sudden, the wind picks up.

(TONY *points to* RYAN, *who begins rubbing his hands together. He reminds* RYAN *to include the audience.* RYAN *gets the audience to join him.* TONY *looks pleased and gives him the thumbs up.* RYAN *keeps doing his part without stopping.*)

TONY *(continuing his story)*: We looked up and noticed the clouds were starting to roll in. Well, we didn't really think anything of it and just continued to enjoy ourselves. Then, suddenly, the wind picked up some more. *(He motions* RYAN *to increase the wind.)* And then it happened. Slowly but surely, it started to sprinkle. *(*TONY *turns to* LAURA *and points to her, showing her the snaps.* LAURA *starts snapping, leading the audience in her part.* TONY *continues his story.)* Oh, man! It wasn't too bad, but we thought we should start to gather our things up. So we were taking our time, moving everything out of the rain, when out of nowhere came some heavy rain!

*(*TONY *points to* KAT, *who begins to slap her hands on her thighs. Just as she begins, leading the audience,* DREW *bursts in with clapping and yelling.)*

DREW *(yelling and clapping)*: Whooo! Man, that sounds so cool! I love it!

TONY *(stopping everyone and moving toward* DREW*)*: Drew! What are you doing?

DREW *(laughing)*: That sounded so cool! It sounded like it was raining!

TONY *(exasperated)*: Yeah, I know! That's the point! What's up with the yelling? I never told you to yell!

DREW: Sorry, I just got excited!

TONY *(a bit frustrated)*: We've got to start over. *(He moves back to the right side of the stage, standing near* RYAN.*)* Now, Drew, please. Wait until I cue you!

DREW: OK.

TONY *(starting his story over again)*: Grandma's stirring the potato salad. My brother and I are playing football. Out of nowhere, the wind picks up. *(He motions to* RYAN, *who begins the wind again.)* We didn't really think anything of it when all of a sudden it started to sprinkle. *(He taps* LAURA *on the shoulder, and she begins to snap, leading the audience with her.)* So, we thought maybe we should gather our things up while we waited for it to pass. We were getting all our things when out of nowhere it started to rain really hard. *(He points to* KAT, *who begins to slap her hands on her thighs, the audience following her.)* Oh great! We hurried to grab our stuff, and then the downpour hit. *(He motions* KAT *to stomp her feet on the ground while she slaps her hands.* KAT *does so, and the audience follows her.)* We yelled, running for cover, leaving everything behind, and by the time we got to shelter, it happened! *(He points* to DREW, *who eagerly begins his thunderclaps, leading the audience.)* Oh, it was amazing! It was thundering, and everything increased *(motioning everyone to get louder)*, and it was so beautiful! So we just stood there and enjoyed it.

(TONY lets the storm continue for a few seconds. Everyone continues each part, watching TONY for instruction.)

TONY *(slowing DREW down)*: And then the thunder became more sporadic. And finally, the thunder stopped. *(DREW stops.)* The downpour lessened until it was just rain. *(He slows KAT down, motioning her to stop stomping her feet.)* It was beautiful. The rain continued to die down until there were only a few sprinkles. *(He stops KAT, lets the sprinkles continue for a couple seconds, then stops LAURA.)* The wind decreased. *(He slows RYAN down, then directs him to stop.)* Then it was calm.

(Everything is silent for a moment until DREW comments on how cool the storm was. TONY tells the THREE AUDIENCE MEMBERS they can return to their seats. They leave, and TONY resumes his earlier conversation with DREW.)

DREW *(as the others leave)*: Tony, that was cool!

TONY *(agreeing)*: Wasn't it? I loved how it sounded. It sounded so real.

DREW: Yeah. Let me tell you, I was really excited about the thunder. It was great. Well, it hurt my hands because I was clapping so hard, but I think I was pretty good at it.

TONY *(looking expectantly at DREW)*: So, you got it?

DREW: Yeah, it was a thunderstorm. I got it. I said it was cool.

TONY: Yeah, but more than that-did you get why it was a thunderstorm?

DREW: Uh, because that's what we were supposed to make. I get it.

TONY: Remember what we were talking about before? You know, before we made the thunderstorm?

DREW *(confused)*: Sure.

TONY: Remember? The whole conversation about purpose . . . timing . . .

DREW (*slightly annoyed*): Yeah. What about it?

TONY: We were talking about purpose and timing.

DREW: Yes, I know. God is giving me stuff to do, and I want to do it. I'm frustrated.

TONY (*giving* DREW *a curious look*): Yes. That's the whole point of what we just did. (*He pauses.*) Am I talking to a brick wall? OK, listen. The storm was cool, right?

DREW: Yeah.

TONY: Well, it was cool because everything was in its place. That's why it was effective. I specifically picked you to be the thunder. I knew how you were going to fit into the story.

DREW: OK.

TONY: You know how sometimes you jumped in and just started clapping? We had to stop and go back to the beginning of the story.

DREW: Yeah.

TONY: Well, sometimes God has to do the same thing with us. You know what I mean? When we don't do our parts in the right time, it throws things off.

DREW: Yeah, I guess. But I don't understand why it can't just be my turn now.

TONY: Because-everything has a place, even in a storm.

(TONY *and* DREW *pause for a moment then exit.*)

You Can't Be Me

by onetimeblind

Running Time: Approximately 6 minutes

Theme: Each person has something unique that God has given him or her, and only in that uniqueness can they bring the most glory to God

Scripture References: Jeremiah 1:5; Romans 9:17 (NIV)

Synopsis: Two friends are given encouraging cards by a third friend. The cards include qualities the third friend admires in each of the others. One friend decides she doesn't like the qualities others see in her and determines to act like someone she's not. After seeing the "new" her, the third friend indicates how much he values her just the way she is.

Cast: KAT
        LAURA
        DREW
        RYAN
        TONY

Props: Two cards
        Bag of candy
        T-shirt

Setting: DREW finds LAURA and KAT to give them cards he made for them. LAURA and KAT are just hanging out.

(KAT *and* LAURA *walk on-stage, talking about the weather.* KAT'S *personality is outgoing, with lots of passion and intensity in her voice and movements. She uses her hands a lot when she speaks, making wide motions in the air and emphasizing things when she's excited.* LAURA *is much more reserved, standing in place as she talks, not using her hands and acting very sweet-natured.)*

KAT *(excitedly)*: Can you believe this weather?

LAURA *(agreeing)*: I know. It's been so nice!

KAT: Totally nice! I think we should take a walk later. What do you think?

(KAT and LAURA continue to talk about the weather as DREW enters from SR.)

DREW *(cheerfully)*: Hey guys! I'm so glad I found you! I have something for you.

KAT *(loudly)*: What? You're kidding!

LAURA *(smiling at DREW)*: What do you mean?

DREW: Well, I've been reading this book about friendship, and you guys are some of my best friends.

KAT: Whoa! Thanks. That's so awesome!

DREW: Well, in this book it talks about, you know, the qualities of your friends, and what you admire about them, and how you should tell them.

LAURA: Really? That sounds neat.

DREW: Yeah, it is! So, I got some cards for you and wrote down a few qualities I admire about you. You know, things that set you apart from everyone else I know. You're special to me and I want you to know. I appreciate you just the way you are. *(He hands each of them a card.)*

KAT *(passionately, with excitement)*: Wow! That is so nice!

LAURA *(again smiling at DREW)*: Yeah, that's really sweet of you!

DREW *(shrugging)*: Well, you don't have to read them now. It's kind of embarrassing. But I hope you like them. I'll see you later. *(DREW exits SR.)*

LAURA *(sweetly)*: Can you believe that? He is so thoughtful! *(She starts to read her card, notices what it says, and acts flattered but a little bit bummed, quickly closing her card and moving on to some other topic.)*

KAT *(noticing LAURA reading)*: Well, I'm going to read mine now if you're going to read yours! *(She opens her card and begins to read it.)*

LAURA: Hmmm. Yep, this is nice. So about the weather–it sure is something out there, isn't it?

KAT *(really emphasizing her words)*: Whoa! This is awesome! *(She uses wide gestures as she speaks.)*

LAURA *(still bummed)*: Yeah, it's nice, isn't it?

KAT *(continuing to emphasize certain words with her wild motions)*: I mean, I never see myself the way other people see me. Like, I never think about what people see until they tell me. And then I think, am I really like that? Because that makes me think about how God must see me and the qualities He's given me. And I never really even knew that I had them! That is just so cool!

LAURA *(looking curious)*: Yeah, it's interesting to see what people think about you. Sometimes it's kind of surprising how other people see you, you know?

KAT *(excitedly)*: Definitely. *(She looks at* LAURA, *slightly puzzled at her hesitance.)* You like your card, right?

LAURA: Yeah, it's great. He picked out such a cute one for me.

KAT *(interested)*: Well, can I read it?

LAURA *(hesitating)*: Oh, you know, it's really no big deal.

KAT: Oh, right. I was just thinking, like, I wonder if Drew sees what I see, you know? So I could read it, then maybe I could tell you what I see.

LAURA: OK, yeah. I guess. *(She hands her card to* KAT.*)*

KAT: Cool. Well, you can read mine. Here. *(She hands her card to* LAURA.*)*

*(*KAT *and* LAURA *read each other's cards, commenting on how right on they are.)*

LAURA *(sweetly)*: Wow, this is so right. I mean, you have all of the qualities! *(She reads over the card and looks wistfully at* KAT.*)* You really do stand out. Everything on this card perfectly describes you. I wish I had some of your qualities.

KAT *(disbelieving)*: What are you talking about? You have the greatest qualities ever! You're sweet, kind, gentle . . . *(She gets louder.)* Oh man, I wish I could be gentle!

LAURA *(kindly interrupting)*: Yeah, that's what I mean. Everyone always says I'm sweet, but sweet doesn't mean anything. It's so blah.

KAT *(emphatically)*: People say you're sweet because you are sweet! Being sweet is good! It's one of the things I love about you!

LAURA *(looking at* KAT'S *card)*: I don't want to be known as sweet. Sweet is boring. It doesn't stand out.

KAT: But you are sweet! It's part of who you are. No one is sweet in the same way you are. Being sweet is part of your essence.

LAURA *(thinking)*: You know what? If I'm really going to leave a mark in this world, I'm going to have to adopt one of your qualities. *(She looks at* KAT'S *card.)* Like your intensity. Drew says here that you're totally intense, and that's so true! So I'm going to be intense.

KAT: What are you talking about? You can't just have my qualities. They're not a part of you; they're a part of me.

LAURA *(slowly building confidence)*: Listen, I told you, I want my life to mean something. I'll never be anything if I'm only known as the sweet girl. So, I'm going to be intense.

KAT *(shaking her head in disbelief)*: You can't do that! You're not an intense person!

(As they continue talking, RYAN *enters from SL carrying a bag of candy.)*

RYAN *(eating some candy)*: Hey, guys! Want some candy?

KAT: Hey, Ryan! *(She eyes the bag of candy and gets really excited, using her hands for emphasis as she talks.)* Where did you get that candy?

*(*KAT *reaches to take a piece of candy from him as* LAURA *cuts in, imitating* KAT'S *words and movements.)*

LAURA *(pushing past* KAT, *using her arms for emphasis and speaking excitedly)*: Yeah, Ryan! Where did you get that candy?

RYAN *(looking slightly confused)*: Uh, Drew gave it to me. It was pretty nice of him.

KAT *(moving back toward* RYAN, *giving* LAURA *an irritated look then talking excitedly again to* RYAN*)*: No way! Do you have any red pieces? *(She again emphasizes certain words with her hands in the air.)* I love the red pieces!

LAURA (*still in "acting" mode, pushing* KAT *out of the way again*): Oh, yeah, do you have any red pieces? I love the red ones!

RYAN (*with an uncomfortable laugh*): Uh, yeah, there are some red ones.

LAURA (*passionately*): Great! And blue–do you have blue? (*She puts her hand over her heart.*) I love the blue ones too! This is so great!

RYAN (*looking curiously at* LAURA *and laughing*): You feeling OK, Laura?

KAT (*rolling her eyes*): She's not herself today. (*She smiles at* RYAN.)

RYAN (*still rather confused, he starts to walk away, toward SL*): Oh, OK. Well, I guess I'll see you guys later. (*He walks off SL.*)

LAURA (*calling loudly after* RYAN): Yeah, you bet. And if you have more candy to get rid of, you just come right back here and share with us because we love candy! (*She punches the air and gives a little "whoohoo!"*)

KAT (*taking* LAURA *by the shoulders*): Laura, what are you doing?

LAURA (*looking innocently at* KAT, *speaking sweetly*): I'm being myself!

KAT (*using her hands for emphasis, speaking loudly*): No, you are not being yourself! You're acting out of control! You're flailing your arms around like a mad woman! I mean, seriously, who acts like that?

LAURA (*again in her normal sweet voice*): I told you, I want to leave a mark in this world, and I'm not going to do it by being sweet. I have to become intense.

KAT (*passionately*): And I told you that's ridiculous!

(*As they talk,* TONY *enters from SR.*)

TONY (*excitedly*): There you are! Pizza party at my place–seven o'clock!

KAT (*intensely*): Hey, Tony! No way, I love pizza!

LAURA (*again acting intense and imitating* KAT): No way, Tony! (*She pushes* KAT *out of the way.*) I love pizza!

TONY (*looking a little confused at* LAURA'S *outburst*): Oh, well, hey. How's it going?

LAURA *(yelling)*: We are great! *(She jumps up and down.)* The greatness is just bubbling up . . .

KAT *(interrupting)*: Look, whatever you order, make sure you get pepperoni–

LAURA *(imitating KAT)*: Pepperoni . . .

KAT *(giving LAURA an exasperating look)*: And pineapple . . .

LAURA *(gain interrupting)*: And pineapple. I love pineapple!

TONY *(sort of chuckling)*: Uh, yeah, OK.

LAURA: You know what? I love, love, love pizza!

TONY: Oh, well, me too!

KAT *(interrupting and ushering TONY toward SL)*: OK, well, thanks for letting us know about the party, Tony. We'll catch up with you in a little while.

TONY *(puzzled)*: OK, then. I'll see you later.

(TONY walks offstage left as LAURA yells after him.)

LAURA *(yelling and using large arm movements)*: See you later, Tony! Thanks for telling us about the party. We'll see you at seven!

KAT *(pulling LAURA back to her)*: What are you doing? What's wrong with you?

LAURA *(sweetly yet a bit defensively)*: I'm being intense–I'm being myself! This is not easy, you know.

Kat: I told you, you're sweet. You are not an intense person.

LAURA *(again in her sweet, normal voice)*: I am now! Intense people stand out. *(She pauses.)* Look, if I'm going to do this, I need your support. I want to leave a mark in this world.

KAT: You are leaving a mark!

LAURA *(ignoring her)*: It's really hard to make such a complete turnaround. If I'm going to pull it off, I really need to concentrate. *(She smiles sweetly at* KAT.*)* I mean, I don't know if you've ever realized this, but it's not easy being you.

KAT *(exasperated)*: That's because you're not supposed to be me! You're supposed to be you!

*(*LAURA *sees* DREW *entering from SR and runs over to him.)*

LAURA *(loudly)*: Whoa, Drew, thank you for the note! That was so cool!

DREW *(laughing)*: Hey!

KAT *(trying to get a word in)*: Um . . .

LAURA *(very loudly and intensely)*: That was so nice of you! We loved the notes! *(She lets out a little "whoop!")*

DREW *(confused)*: Uh, good.

*(*KAT *moves closer to* DREW, *moving* LAURA *further toward SL. She takes her card back from* LAURA, *hands* LAURA'S *card to* DREW, *and begins to leave.)*

KAT *(rolling her eyes at* LAURA*)*: Yeah, thanks for the card, Drew. That was really great. *(She walks offstage.)*

LAURA *(repeating her excitement, moving around and waving her arms)*: Yea, that was great! Hey, did you see Tony? Tony's having a pizza party. Do you know how much I love pizza? I mean, loooovvveee pizza!

DREW *(confused, looking at* LAURA*)*: What are you doing?

LAURA *(pausing then again speaking animatedly)*: I'm, um . . . I'm looking forward to the pizza party! Because everybody's going to be there, and you know what that means–it's gonna be fun, fun, fun!

DREW: OK, Laura. You're freakin' me out.

LAURA: Oh, no, I'm just excited to see you because you really started my day off right!

DREW: Fine . . . but what are you doing?

LAURA *(punching* DREW *on the arm)*: You know how to make me happy!

DREW *(holding his arm)*: Ow! What's wrong with you?

LAURA: Nothing! I'm just, uh, feeling a little more intense today, you know? *(She pushes her hands into the air for emphasis.)*

DREW *(confused)*: OK, you're not acting like yourself. What's wrong? I mean, normally you're just nice and sweet . . .

LAURA *(sighing, then speaking in her normal, sweet voice, more reserved and defeated)*: But I don't want to be nice and sweet.

DREW: What do you mean, you don't want to be sweet?

LAURA: I mean, it's so boring. I don't stand out at all. I don't make a difference to anyone.

DREW: Wait . . .

LAURA *(interrupting)*: I mean, if that's what people see in me, I need to make some changes.

DREW *(showing her the card)*: Laura, that's not the only thing on here. There's so much to you! Look . . .

LAURA *(interrupting again)*: If that's all you see, I obviously don't stand out.

DREW *(holding* LAURA'S *card)*: No, I see a lot in you. In fact, you're the only you that I know. I mean, when I walk into a room, and I'm having a bad day or something, I know you will always cheer me up. I know you're always going to be nice to me, and that means something. No one else is like that. You are the only friend I have who is like you!

LAURA *(sadly, in her normal, sweet voice)*: Look, Drew, it's fine for you to think that, but being sweet doesn't mean anything to me.

DREW *(softly)*: Well, it might not mean anything to you *(hands her the card)*, but it means something to me.

*(*DREW *exits SR.* LAURA *is left alone holding the card. After a brief pause, she exits SL.)*

Who Am I?

Words and Music by
MARK HALL

1. Who am I _____ that the
(2. Who am I) _____ that the

Lord of all the earth   would
eyes that see my sin   would

care to know my name,   would
look on me with love   and

care to feel my hurt?
watch me rise a - gain?

ev - er wan - d'ring heart?_____
calm the storm_____ in me?_____

Not be - cause of who____ I am,____

____ but be - cause of what____ You've done,____

44

28

not be - cause of what___ I've done,___

F♯/A♯ G♯m7

CD: 17 *1st time*
CD: 19 *2nd time*

30

Opt. harmony both times

but be - cause of who___ You are.___

F♯/A♯ E

32

f

I am a flow - er quick - ly fad -

F♯ E/F♯ B F♯/A♯

f

35

- ing, here to - day and gone___ to - mor -

G♯m7 F♯

I am Yours,____

I am Yours.____

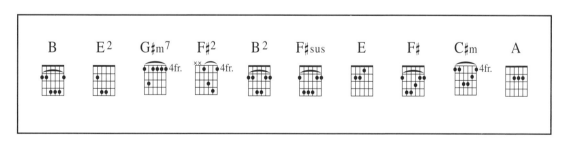

Spoken Word

by Darryl Canty and Ryan McCullough

Running Time: Approximately 4 minutes

Theme: Purpose

Scripture References: Proverbs 2:1-9; Philippians 2:13 (NIV)

Cast: SPEAKER

Safety in crowds and purpose in groups
The crowd moves in a herd or a flock like birds
I'm in the center of it all-I know where I'm going
Things seem to be flowing
No thought or work, I just glide or coast
There is purpose here-the thing I like the most
Like a big group at an amusement park-staying till dark-
We stay together only so long
Then somehow I'm getting separated-cut off
I stumble around the park not knowing where I am going
What do I ride next? The corkscrew or Vortex
Before I know it I've squandered time and day
Wandered and squandered, Ah, these thoughts I've pondered
I've pondered my "wanderedness" and wandered my wilderness
I'm one step closer to nowhere *(pause)* One step closer to nowhere
And it's getting me angry and it's making me sick
I'm in the thick-separated from my people, my clique
Who am I without the group
Who is Joey without 'NSYNC or 182 without the Blink
Take us from our groups and we don't know what to think
I have a part in this play but I don't know what to say
I know the title, but what's my part? Where do I fit?
What's my line?
Line, please! Just give me my line!
I need the line that is mine-for me and me alone

I need to be shown. Director, what is my line?

But silence-nothing. He won't give me what's mine.

One step closer to nowhere-one closer-one step

Step in for me, please-I'm becoming a wreck!

Am I supposed to know what to do?

Should I know where I am going?

The Lord left me-head shaking-mouth gaping

People passing with purpose seem to know where they're headed

On my right, on my left-seeming to know their part.

Criminal cruel! It's crushing, seeing them rushing-off to their purpose

Their place-their space

And not a one-space-fits-all but one that is just for them

Break me! Break it! I'm Broken!

I got this feeling I'm choking

And I ain't going nowhere-nothing but silence to share *(pause)*

One step closer to nowhere, one closer, one step

One second at a time to a purpose that's mine

Seconds turn to minutes-minutes turn to hours

Men turn to power when purpose is made clear

Second by second you lead me, step by step, not year by year

Moment by moment you are a lamp to my feet

With every tick that passes I'm one step closer to knowing

One second, one letter, one word-sweetest that I've ever heard

Each coming at its time

Vision waking me up like a clock radio

Not the one that I picked but the one He gave me though

Steps closer to nowhere become steps to knowing

But I couldn't have found my way without losing it

I couldn't have kept my ego without bruising it

Without breaking off

Not going the way I was shown but blazing new trails

Trails that only I was meant to blaze

I'm called to cut through the haze

Find the path through the maze

Accomplishing only what I could do.

I Still Believe

Words and Music by
JEREMY CAMP

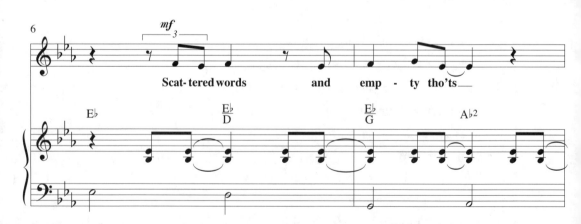

Scat- tered words   and   emp - ty tho'ts___

56

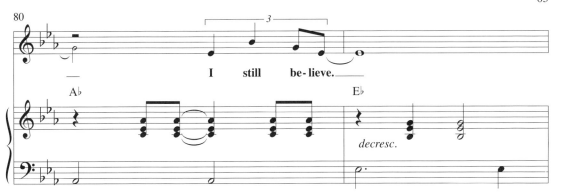

I still be-lieve.

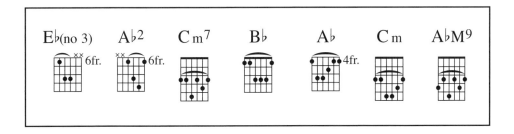

Created to Worship

Words and Music by
VICKY BEECHING

You formed us from the dust,

You breathed Your breath in us.

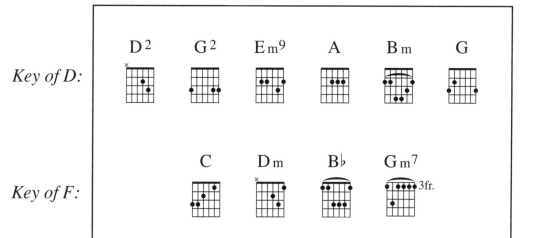

Prove It to Me

By onetimeblind

Running Time: Approximately 4 minutes

Themes: Doubt, Faith, Why do bad things happen if God is so loving?

Scripture References: John 4:48; John 20:29 (NIV)

Synopsis: The DEVIL addresses the audience, challenging them to prove their belief in God.

Cast: DEVIL

Props: One black pair of sunglasses (used to represent the DEVIL, who distorts the Light)

(The DEVIL enters wearing a pair of sunglasses to represent who he is. He stands center stage and presents the audience with a barrage of questions.)

DEVIL *(in a slightly mocking tone)*: So, you think God loves you, huh? You really think God loves you? *(He looks out at the audience, almost daring them to contradict him.)* Prove it to me. Huh? Prove it to me! Oh, because it says so in the Bible? It's just a book. How do you really know it's real? Prove to me He loves you. Oh, because Jesus died for you? He loved you this much *(stretching out his arms in cross formation)*. That's a safe, Sunday school answer. But you don't know for sure. You don't know if it's real. So I ask-does He love you? Prove it to me. If there's love in the world, if God really loves you, why are there "natural" disasters that kill so many thousands of people? Why do we have a disease called AIDS that is ravaging this planet? If God is a God of love, why does He allow suicide bombers to take the lives of innocent women and children in His name? Does that sound like love to you?

(He paces slowly back and forth on the stage as he speaks. He stops and again dares the audience to give him the answers to his questions.)

DEVIL *(a bit more taunting)*: You think He really loves you? Prove it to me. If He loves you so much, why do people always make fun of you? Why do so many marriages get ripped apart? Why are people always stabbing you in the back and lying to you every time you turn around? If God loves you, why do the people you love leave you? That doesn't sound like love to me.

(The DEVIL *again paces across the stage as he briefly pauses to let his questioning sink in to people's minds.)*

DEVIL *(a little bolder)*: If He loves you so much, then prove it to me. Prove to me He loves you because if He loves you so much, why does it seem like He doesn't want to be close to you? Why does He keep putting things in your way-putting things in between you and Him? Why, if God loves you so much, do you constantly struggle, day in and day out? Why does God always put you in a place where you are completely alone? *(He pauses then digs the last question in deeply, emphasizing the idea of futility people feel in their lives.)* If God really loves you, why is it that you spend every single day asking questions you will never get the answers to?

(He stands with a smirk on his face, as if he knows no one can dispute him.)

DEVIL *(satisfied)*: Huh. That doesn't sound like love to me. *(He pauses again then speaks the next phrases with increasing adamancy.)* You say God loves you-then prove it to me. Prove it to me! *(He pauses one last time, piercing the audience with his gaze, then continues in a softer, still mocking, tone.)* If you can't prove it to me, how can you prove it to yourself?

(The DEVIL *gives a satisfied smirk and walks offstage.)*

All You Will See

by one**time**blind

Running Time: Approximately 6 minutes

Themes: Intimacy with Jesus, moving to a deeper level with Him

Scripture References: I John 15:4, 9; James 4:8 (NIV)

Synopsis: JESUS appeals to KAT to come closer to Him, but she is afraid of what she might
see in herself when she looks into JESUS' eyes.

Cast: JESUS
       KAT
       DEVIL

Props: Journal with pen
       Chair

Setting: KAT is sitting on a chair at center stage, writing in her journal, when JESUS comes out
to meet her.

*(KAT walks onstage, sits in a chair, opens her journal and begins writing. She speaks out
loud as she writes, giving the audience the impression that they can "hear" her writing.)*

KAT *(writing and speaking)*: Wednesday, the 27th. Well, today has been some kind of day.
    I have had so much to do. I don't even remember what all I've done today because
    I've been so busy. *(She continues writing/talking about her day, listing her thoughts
    in typical journal fashion.)*

*(As KAT is writing, JESUS enters from stage right and walks up to the right side of KAT'S
chair, leaving a few feet between them.)*

JESUS *(softly but firmly)*: Kathlene, it's time for you to come closer. *(He looks expectantly
    at KAT.)*

(KAT is slightly startled and noticeably uncomfortable at JESUS' sudden appearance.)

KAT (*mumbling a bit*): Oh! Wow. Hey, Jesus, it's been awhile. I'd love to talk, but I'm a bit busy right now. (KAT *avoids looking* JESUS *in the eyes, as she is obviously uneasy.*)

JESUS (*firmly, with expectancy in His voice*): I want to be close to you, Kat. It's time for you to come closer to Me. I want you to look at Me.

(KAT *continues to avert her eyes from* JESUS' *while attempting to avoid direct conversation with Him. She again pulls her journal in front of her and begins journaling, hoping* JESUS *will go away.*)

JESUS (*slightly confused by her avoidance of Him*): Kat, I want to be close to you. I want you to look into My eyes.

KAT: Oh, Jesus! Are You still here? I thought You had left. (*She continues to stare at her journal, a bit uncertain as to whether He will let her be.*)

JESUS (*more insistently*): Kat, seriously, just look at Me and talk to Me! I want to be close to you! There's so much I have for you if you'll just look at Me. You and I are supposed to be intimate.

KAT (*speaking quickly*): Look, Jesus, I'm sorry, but please refrain from using the word "intimate." I'm not comfortable with that-especially not with You!

JESUS (*slightly confused yet a bit amused*): Who told you being intimate is bad? That's not true! Being intimate is something God designed. It's meant to be holy. Just look at Me, and you'll see. Let's take this to a deeper level. Come closer. (*He looks at* KAT, *waiting for her to look at Him.*)

KAT (*in a final attempt to get Him to leave*): Jesus, please go away! I'm fine where I am and comfortable with what I am doing. Please just go and leave me be. (*She again starts to write in her journal.*)

(JESUS *has finally had enough and puts His hand over* KAT'S *journal, stopping her from writing and forcing her to pay attention to Him. He begins a dialogue that gives the feeling they've been in this place before.*)

JESUS (*intently*): I want to take you deeper, Kat, but you resist Me. Every time. We never get past this point because you're too scared. It's time. It's time for you to come closer.

(KAT *continues in avoidance mode. She laughs, talks about her sweaty palms, asks silly questions like "where's the bathroom," tries to change the subject, fidgets, etc. As she goes on and on,* JESUS *continues to tell her He wants to be close to her. After a few excuses from her, He takes her journal and places it on the floor in front of Him. At this point, the* DEVIL *enters from stage left, walking slowly and coming up behind* KAT. *He walks slow enough to give* JESUS *time to say His next few lines before moving.)*

(Note: The DEVIL'S *role in this skit is silent. His presence brings tension, conflict, and urgency to the situation. The* DEVIL *interacts silently with* JESUS, *who sees him, and with* KAT, *who does not. He gets very close to them, circling, mocking, and prowling throughout the entire piece.)*

KAT *(suddenly alert, staring at her journal on the floor in disbelief)*: What are You doing? That's my journal. You can't just take my journal!

JESUS: There! That's better. You're talking to Me!

KAT *(still looking away, off in the distance, and now a bit miffed)*: I was talking to You before.

JESUS: No, you weren't. You were avoiding Me. Now look at Me. I want you to come close.

KAT: No! I can't.

JESUS *(again firmly, yet with gentleness)*: Kat, I want you to come closer.

KAT *(sighs)*: Fine. *(She moves her chair just a bit closer, still looking away from* JESUS.) There, I'm closer.

JESUS *(waiting, looking at the* DEVIL *as he nears* KAT): Closer. Kat, this is urgent. It's important.

KAT *(exasperated)*: Fine! *(She moves her chair a little closer, still looking away from* JESUS.) There, happy now? *(She sits there for a second, thinking.)* Jesus, this is a good distance, so I have a great idea. When You see me getting too far away, You let me know.

JESUS *(moving to the left side of* KAT, *blocking the* DEVIL *as he attempts to get close to her)*: You're already too far away.

(During the next few lines, the DEVIL *moves to the right side of* KAT, *kneeling down beside her and playing with her hair, smiling in her face, silently taunting her.)*

*(*KAT *ignores* JESUS *and reaches over to grab her journal off the floor.)*

JESUS *(immediately as* KAT *reaches)*: Too far.

KAT: I'm just reaching for my . . .

JESUS *(emphatically)*: Too far.

KAT: Jesus, I'm just trying to get my stuff! Can't I even go anywhere?

JESUS *(firmly)*: Come closer.

KAT *(frustrated)*: Jesus, I'm fine where I am! I don't need to be any closer!

JESUS *(immediately)*: I want you closer to Me. I've seen you stare into your own eyes and loath what you see. Look into My eyes, and you'll see who you really are. We're meant to be close. Very close. It's in My reflection that you'll see yourself as you really are, as you were created to be.

KAT *(with a tinge of bitterness as she stares off into the distance)*: You're right, Jesus. I have looked in my eyes, and I know what's there. It's a constant reminder of something I hate.

(The DEVIL *stands up, chuckling silently.* JESUS *moves back to the right side of* KAT, *once again cutting off the* DEVIL'S *access to her. The* DEVIL *taunts* JESUS, *getting in His face, feeling confident of his own power.* JESUS *knows the* DEVIL *is there but focuses His main attention on* KAT.)*

JESUS *(softly)*: I want you to look at Me.

KAT *(with resistance in her voice)*: I'm not comfortable with that, with looking at You! If I do that, all I'll be reminded of is what I'm not. You don't understand. I know what's in my heart; I know what I think; I know what I've done. If I look in Your eyes, all I will see is my sin.

JESUS *(looking at her, conveying His sincerity)*: All you will see is Me.

KAT (*trying to talk Him out of His idea*): You don't want to be that close to Me. You can't. I'm not what You think I am. I'm not who You think I am!

JESUS (*again insistently*): All you will see is Me.

KAT (*frustrated, still looking away*): That is not true, Lord! It's not true. I know how imperfect I am. I have flaws. I have baggage-loads and loads of baggage. What I am is not a pretty sight.

JESUS: Kat . . . all you will see is . . .

KAT (*interrupting*): Listen to me! It won't be the way You have it played out in Your mind. I told You, I'm not perfect. Looking into Your eyes would only reveal to me everything I am not.

JESUS (*emphatically*): Kat . . .

KAT (*again interrupting, standing up, frustrated*): Look, Jesus, I can't do that! I am full of flaws. There is nothing good about me. I can't look at You because if I do . . . (*she pauses, feeling defeated, then continues in a soft voice*) if I look in Your eyes . . . if I do that . . .

(*As KAT says the previous lines, JESUS eyes the DEVIL, who is standing very close between them. He pushes the DEVIL back firmly, confidently, with His left hand, then says His next line.*)

JESUS (*gently but firmly, speaking to KAT*): When you look in My eyes . . . (*He pulls her toward Him so she is standing face to face with Him, about three inches apart. As soon as KAT is planted in front of Him, He continues with His next line.*) all you will see.

(*Several seconds of silence pass as KAT and JESUS stand face to face, staring at each other. As they stand there, the DEVIL fades offstage, walking off stage right, staring at them as he leaves. The time KAT and JESUS stand silently should be long enough to make the audience feel uncomfortable, about twenty to thirty seconds or so. After enough time passes, dialogue begins again.*)

KAT (*staring into JESUS' eyes in awe*): I see.

JESUS (*smiling*): Yes. (*Still facing each other, He takes* KAT'S *hand and places it over His heart.*) Do you feel that?

KAT (*with joy and wonder*): Your heart.

JESUS (*correcting her*): My Love. I love you as the Father loves Me. Remain in Me as I remain in you. Remain in My love. (*He takes* KAT'S *hand and moves it to her own heart, placing His hand over hers. As He moves her hand, she follows with her eyes and moves her head, looking downward toward the hands on her heart, and closes her eyes.*)

KAT (*flatly, as her hand is placed over her own heart*): My heart.

JESUS (*again correcting her*): My Love. It never leaves you. It's always right there. Even when you can't see Me. Even when you think I'm not here, I am. I am with you.

(KAT *is still looking down, with her eyes closed and both their hands over her heart.*)

JESUS (*softly*): Remember. And know that I am here. (*He removes His hand from hers and watches her tenderly as He walks off stage right, continuing to whisper, "Remember. Remember. Remember."*)

(KAT *keeps her eyes closed, savoring the moment, then slowly opens her eyes and looks up. She breathes in a breath of reverence and breathes out a moment of certainty, slightly nodding her head, then walks softly offstage.*)

Note: Depending upon the use of this skit, it may be done as is, or KAT'S *part may lead into an invitation after she raises her head at the end. For an invitation, she would breathe in her moment of reverence, exhale her certainty in Christ's love, then begin speaking to the audience from her heart, offering them an opportunity to move to a deeper, more intimate place with Jesus.*

Sweep Me Away

Words and Music by
CHARLIE HALL, KENDAL COMBES,
BRIAN BERGMAN, TODD CROMWELL
and WILL HUNT

1. Sud-den-ly I feel__ You hold - ing me,
2. Sud-den-ly I feel__ Your hand__ in mine,

3. Sud-den-ly I feel__ You lead - ing me,
4. Sud-den-ly I feel__ Your heart__ in mine,

Opt. harmony both times

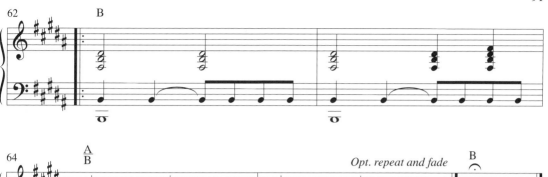

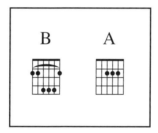

Grace Flows Down

(Instrumental Version)*
To be used during Communion

Music by
DAVID BELL, LOUIE GIGLIO
and ROD PADGETT

* An MP3 of this Performance Track may be purchased at www.lillenas.com.
** Guitar fretboard symbols found at the end of "Grace Flows Down" page 101.

Grace Flows Down

Words and Music by
DAVID BELL, LOUIE GIGLIO
and ROD PADGETT

down and cov - ers me.

me. It cov - ers me,

It cov - ers

me, It cov - ers

And cov - ers____ me.____

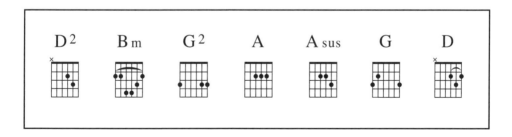

How Great Is Our God

Words and Music by
CHRIS TOMLIN, JESSE REEVES
and ED CASH

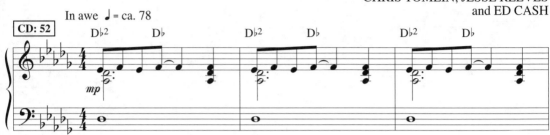

Sing with me,___ how___ great is our God!___

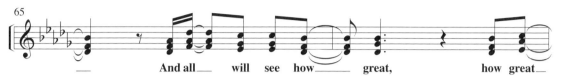

And all___ will see how___ great, how great___

is our God!___

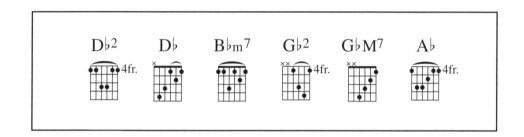

D♭2   D♭   B♭m7   G♭2   G♭M7   A♭

Birthright

Helpful Links

Lillenas Drama
www.lillenasdrama.com

onetimeblind
www.onetimeblind.com

EMI
www.emicmg.com

The Visible School
www.visibleschool.com

Barefoot Ministries
www.barefootministries.com